Rough Guides

25 Ultimate experiences

Canada

Make the most of your time on Earth

ROUGH GUIDES

25 YEARS 1982–2007

NEW YORK • LONDON • DELHI

Contents

Introduction

EXPERIENCES have always been at the heart of the Rough Guide concept. A group of us began writing the books **25 years ago** (hence this celebratory mini series) and wanted to share the kind of travels we had been doing ourselves. It seems bizarre to recall that in the early 1980s, travel was very much a minority pursuit. Sure, there was a lot of tourism around, and that was reflected in the guidebooks in print, which traipsed around the established sights with scarcely a backward look at the local population and their life. We wanted to change all that: to put a country or a city's popular culture centre stage, to highlight the clubs where you could hear local music, drink with people you hadn't come on holiday with, watch the local football, join in with the festivals. And of course we wanted to push travel a bit further, inspire readers with the confidence and knowledge to break away from established routes, to find pleasure and excitement in remote islands, or desert routes, or mountain treks, or in street culture.

Twenty-five years on, that thinking seems pretty obvious: we all want to experience something real about a destination, and to seek out travel's **ultimate experiences**. Which is exactly where these **25 books** come in. They are not in any sense a new series of guidebooks. We're happy with the series that we already have in print. Instead, the **25s** are a collection of ideas, enthusiasms and inspirations: a selection of the very best things to see or do – and not just before you die, but now. Each selection is gold dust. That's the brief to our writers: there is no room here for the average, no space fillers. Pick any one of our selections and you will enrich your travelling life.

But first of all, take the time to browse. Grab a half dozen of these books and let the ideas percolate … and then begin making your plans.

Mark Ellingham
Founder & Series Editor, Rough Guides

Ultimate
experiences
Canada

cycling around
Stanley Park
in Vancouver

01

More so than any other Canadian city, nature-loving Vancouver embraces the ethos "two wheels good, four wheels bad". And cycling around Stanley Park's breathtaking shoreline, you're bound to start invoking it yourself. It could be as Mount Baker comes into view, rearing up from the horizon like a glaciated castle. Or as a lone racoon scampers across the bicycle path, seducing you with its big guilty eyes before darting into the rainforest. Or as you spot a couple sharing an ice cream while watching the sun set from a beachside log.

Whatever the case, it might be the best place to discover what the city is all about: the cycle path that goes along the Seawall sketches the great green heart of Vancouver. Jutting out into the ocean from just beyond the shimmering glass skyscrapers of downtown, Stanley Park is the largest urban park in North America, a 1000-acre oasis of towering forests, lakes, manicured gardens, marshland and beaches.

Come winter, when Vancouver's outdoor types relocate to the ski slopes of Grouse, Cyprus and Whistler, cyclists can enjoy this natural splendour in relative solitude. On a scorching summer Sunday however, the Seawall is chock-full of children whizzing past on training wheels, students trying to balance on roller blades and fitness fanatics peddling their way to an invisible finishing line.

On such days, it is wise to leave the path most travelled to cycle deep into the park's shaded interior, past lofty hemlock, Douglas fir and cedar trees, past colourful totem poles and out to serene and secluded Beaver Lake. Here – surrounded by water lilies – you'll declare your undying love for the city, and the two good wheels you rode in on.

NEED TO KNOW

Cycling the path that traces Stanley Park's 10.5-kilometre Seawall takes about an hour; you must ride in a counterclockwise loop. Bicycle shops on Denman Street in downtown Vancouver hire out bikes from C$5 an hour.

sea kayaking in the
Mingan Archipelago

On the map, the Mingan Archipelago looks like a trail of biscuit crumbs scattered in the Gulf of St Lawrence. From the vantage point of your sea kayak, cruising through the channels that separate this collection of forty uninhabited islands and nearly a thousand islets and reefs, it's a much different story. For one, it's impossible to miss the tall rock monoliths that guard the bays. The sea has worn the rock into smooth curves, and the monoliths look very much like people from a distance, like towers of abandoned flying saucers placed one on top of the other from closer to shore.

02

For another, much of what you're paddling around to see actually lurks beneath the surface. The waters are a feeding ground for the largest mammal on earth, the blue whale, as well as minke, fin, beluga and humpback whales. Keep your eyes trained on the horizon looking for the telltale puff of water vapour blown by a whale as it surfaces. But don't ignore what's right around you: seals pop their heads through the waves, like periscopes, no more than a few strokes away. As if curious, they stare at you with their moustachioed faces and big brown eyes, before disappearing with a flash of silver underbelly.

Beneath your paddles the water is so clear that it magnifies the seabed. Bright orange sea stars, deep red urchins and lime green kelp crust the sea floor, the rock worn into

underwater monoliths or crazy paved ledges. As sunset stains the sea pink and purple, you'll need to pick an island and a beachside campsite. Civilization feels a galaxy away as you laze around the campfire or scramble up a clifftop for a last gaze out at sea, hopeful of spotting the silhouette of a whale against the sinking sun.

NEED TO KNOW

The Mingan Archipelago National Park Reserve of Canada stretches 150km from Longue-Pointe-de-mingan to Aguanish, on the north shore of the Gulf of St Lawrence. The best place to organize a kayaking excursion is Havre-Saint-Pierre, where **Expédition Agaguk** (☎ 418/538-1588, ⓦ www.expedition-agaguk.com) rents equipment and provides guides for trips around the islands. A day-trip costs around C$100, a five-day expedition more like C$500.

03

Prince Edward
Island

It may be Canada's smallest province, but Prince Edward Island has produced an enduring classic of children's literature. Lucy Maud Montgomery, the creator of pig-tailed orphan girl *Anne of Green Gables*, loved the place, describing it as floating "on the waves of the blue gulf, a green seclusion and haunt of ancient peace". Much of the peace went with the arrival of the motor car, but the island is still delightfully rural, its rolling fields studded with timber farmsteads and its coasts dinted by elegiac coves and bays.

Montgomery spent much of her youth in the tiny hamlet of Cavendish and her childhood home – Green Gables House – attracts visitors by the busload. It's a short stroll from the seashore, where a narrow band of low red cliff and marram-covered sand dunes flanks a gorgeous beach, extending as far as the eye can see. With the odd interruption for a cove here and an inlet there, it stretches along the island's north shore for some 40km, dotted with campsites and easy hiking trails. Now protected as the Prince Edward Island National Park, the beach is a beautiful place for long blustery walks in winter and swimming and sunbathing in the summer, and a narrow road running just inland provides easy access by car or bike.

Locals usually take a picnic when they head off to the beach, but in the summertime it's always worth looking out for the island's famous lobster suppers. All along the coast, especially in and around the village of New Glasgow, churches and community halls compete – in a thoroughly neighbourly manner – to lay on the island's best seafood. Montgomery, you sense, would feel right at home.

NEED TO KNOW

A bridge links the New Brunswick mainland with PEI, or you can fly to the island capital, Charlottetown, from most cities in eastern Canada. For further information, consult Ⓦwww.gov.pe.ca/visitorsguide.

Lighting
up the sky in
Montreal

Summer is a celebratory time in Montréal. After the hibernation of winter, Montrealers spill on to the street terraces and fill the parks at the first sign of fine weather. Keen to milk it for all it's worth, the city lays on all sorts of colourful outdoor parties – like the calypso-tinged Cariefiesta and the world's pre-eminent jazz festival – that keep you tapping your feet. But the constant crowd-pleaser just requires you look up: the twice-weekly spectacular fireworks display, which pays tribute to balmy nights in a normally frigid city.

Okay, so the Montréal International Fireworks Competition was not created back in 1985 simply to fête summer, but it has become so synonymous with Montréal's best months that it could well have been. Instead, the idea is to synchronize music and pyrotechnics in order to tell some kind of a story, to create an ephemeral fantasy world above the skies of this atmospheric town. Fireworks companies representing different countries let off their considerable arsenals at La Ronde – an amusement park on an island in the middle of the St. Lawrence River – and the shows are stunningly artistic.

The thousands upon thousands of wheels, candles, fountains and rockets that light the night sky are intended to be viewed with the accompanying musical score (broadcast live on local radio). From there it's not too far a leap to imagine Evita disappearing in smoke over the river to the strains of *Don't Cry For Me Argentina* or to take a profusion of red stars and comets set to the soundtrack of *Born Free* to be the rising African sun. Then again, you could just turn off the radio, tilt your head skyward and be thankful that summertime has come.

NEED TO KNOW

The Montréal International Fireworks Competition (Ⓦ www.internationaldesfeuxloto-quebec.com) takes place from mid-June to late July. There are two 30min shows per week on Wednesdays and Saturdays at 10pm. Tickets (C$38–48) are required if you want to see the shows at La Ronde itself.

There are, however, good views for free all over the city: one of the best is next to the Jacques Cartier Bridge on the north bank of the St. Lawrence River.

form a lasting impression at

Niagara Falls

Lake Louise

It's the kind of place you have to see to believe: an impossibly turquoise lake backed by forested slopes, snow-clad mountains and an imposing white glacier. Once this perfect vision is in view, your first instinct will be to take photograph after photograph, as if frightened that the place might suddenly, inexplicably disappear. Your next instinct should be to strike out into the wilderness that surrounds resplendent Lake Louise, jewel of Banff National Park – not just to see the lake from a few more angles, but to conquer some of the most astonishing day-hiking territory in the world.

The immediate area has hours of well-maintained trails. Some are flat and follow the lake's edge, offering images of towering white peaks reflected in serene crystal clear water; others climb up, deep into the forest, to rustic teahouses and smaller shimmering lakes cradled in the mountains. Dazzling views unfold at every switchback. The most strenuous hike takes you on

a twenty-kilometre odyssey to Louise's smaller, scenic rival (hard as that may be to believe), Moraine Lake. Another trail brings you face to-face with the icy, crevassed Victoria Glacier which, every spring, melts and flows into Lake Louise, carrying with it the finely ground glacial silt which gives the lake its emerald hue. Here, you can also watch massive chunks of snow crash from mountainsides, creating almighty booms that reverberate throughout the valley.

NEED TO KNOW

Lake Louise is 57km northwest of Banff and 183km from Calgary. Hiking trails around Lake Louise are accessible from late May to early October, though access is sometimes restricted due to bear alerts. For trail information, visit the Lake Louise Visitor Reception Centre at Samson Mall in Lake Louise Village (☎ 403/522-3833 or 522-1264).

In 1860, thousands watched as Charles Blondin walked a tightrope across Niagara Falls for the third time. Midway, he paused to cook an omelette on a portable grill and then had a marksman shoot a hole through his hat from the *Maid of the Mist* tugboat, 50m below. Suffice to say, the falls simply can't be beat as a theatrical setting.

Like much good theatre, Niagara makes a stupendous first impression, as it crashes over a 52m cliff shrouded in oceans of mist. It's actually two cataracts: tiny Goat Island, which must be one of the wettest places on earth, divides the accelerating water into two channels on either side of the US-Canadian border. The spectacle is, if anything, even more extraordinary in winter, when snow-bent trees edge a jagged armoury of freezing mist and heaped ice blocks.

You won't just be choosing sides – note that the American Falls are but half the width of Canada's Horseshoe Falls – but also how to best see the falls beyond that first impression. A bevy of boats, viewing towers, helicopters, cable cars and even tunnels in the rock-face behind the cascade ensure that every angle is covered.

Two methods are especially thrilling and get you quite near the action: the *Maid of the Mist* boats, which struggle against the cauldron to get as close to the Falls as they dare; and the tunnels of the "Journey Behind the Falls", which lead to points directly behind the waterfall. Either way guarantees that first impression won't be the last one to register.

NEED TO KNOW

Niagara Falls is a two-hour drive south of Toronto; there are also reasonably good train and bus services between the two. The **Maid of the Mist** boats leave every 15–30min and cost C$14. **The Journey Behind the Falls** tour lasts 30–45min and costs C$11.

06

19

Signs boldly reading "Polar Bear Alert – Stop, don't walk in this area" dot the city-limits of Churchill, Manitoba. Beyond them lie wide expanses of the bleak and often-frozen Hudson Bay or the treeless, endlessly flat tundra. It's this location – on the threshold of the two environments – that makes the town the unchallenged "polar bear capital of the world".

Local polar bears spend most of their lives roaming the platform of ice covering the Hudson Bay to hunt seals. But by July the ice melt forces the bears ashore to subsist on berries, lichen, seaweed, mosses and grasses. This brings the animals close to your doorstep; indeed, during the summer the Churchill's Polar Bear Police typically remove over a hundred bears from the town. While this might sound like fun, the reality is quite different: these cuddly-looking bears are the largest land carnivores in existence. They can run at 50km an hour, and kill with a single whack of their foot-wide, clawed paws. And, unaccustomed to humans, they'll quickly size you up as potential prey.

Better to wait until later in the year, from the relative comfort of a tundra buggy – a converted bus that rides high above the

tracking down

polar
bears

in Churchill

ground on giant balloon tires – to do your bear watching. At the beginning of October, around two hundred polar bears gather near town to wait for the bay to freeze. With temperatures beginning to drop below zero and winds gusting up to forty miles an hour, the prime viewing season begins.

Lean and mean from the meager summer diet, male polar bears spend the term sparring with one another for hours on end – standing on their hind legs to throw gentlemanly chest-punches. Females steer well clear of these shenanigans, particularly when with cubs, and spotting a mother lying back on a snowbank nursing

her offspring – making tenderness and brute force temporary bedfellows – is a surprisingly touching scene.

NEED TO KNOW

The simplest way to get to Churchill, in Canada's far north, is to fly from Winnipeg (2 daily, 3hrs 30mins; around C$700) with a carrier like Calm Air (☎204/778-6471; Www.calmair.com); if you have the time and patience the VIA Rail train from Winnipeg is also an option (3 weekly, 34hrs; from C$300; Ⓦwww.viarail.ca). A ride on a tundra buggy costs around C$80 per day.

getting lost within

the walls of
Vieux-Québec

You'd be forgiven for mistaking Canada's most graceful downtown for somewhere in the middle of Europe. Ambling the cobbled streets of a centuries-old walled city, where the views encompass castle turrets and battlefields – and the main language spoken is French – it's easy to feel you've left North America behind. Founded by the French in 1608, Québec City was taken by the English in a 1759 battle just outside the city walls; the victory also won them control of all Canada. The fortifications survive today, making it North America's only walled

city; they mark the boundaries of the old town, or Vieux-Québec. Its lovingly maintained chaotic tangle of streets holds a treasury of historic architecture, fine restaurants and tiny museums. Puttering around its pedestrianized precincts – which are virtually untouched by minimarts, chain stores and fast-food restaurants – is the chief pleasure of a visit here.

The lower town, particularly the Quartier Petit-Champlain – a beautiful warren of narrow lanes and hidden staircases

lined by carefully restored limestone buildings – is a good place to begin an aimless wander. It's easy to idle away hours soaking up the historic charm, listening to buskers and browsing refined boutiques, antique shops and studio-galleries where artists are often at work, before being tempted by the aromas that spill from the doorways of the many old-fashioned restaurants.

Luckily the climbs up and down the steeply sloping streets and staircases around the town help justify indulging

in rich, multicourse meals. After some Québec *foie gras*, local duck, rabbit or wild game, and creamy local cheeses, you'll need to hit the streets again to walk it all off.

NEED TO KNOW

Summer is the obvious time to visit Québec City, but even in winter when temperatures drop comically low, the city is well worth a visit. Vieux-Québec is divided into two sections: Haute-Ville (upper town) and Basse-Ville (lower town).

Dawson City

In the 1890s, rumour spread that the streets of Dawson City were paved with gold. In the most hysterical gold rush stampede the world has ever known, tens of thousands of fortune-seekers packed their bags and headed north for this former patch of moose pasture just below the Arctic Circle. By the time they arrived, most of the claims had been staked, and the brothels, dance halls and theatres of this burgeoning city were busy mining every last cent from the dejected prospectors.

More than a hundred years on, the streets of Dawson City are still not paved with gold. In fact, they're not paved at all, and you need not bother panning for the few flakes of gold left in the creeks just outside of town. Instead, make the trek to

appreciate the rough-and-tumble feel and gold rush-era charm, of which Dawson City still has plenty.

With its historic wooden false-fronted buildings, dirt streets, creaking boardwalks and midnight sun, it's easy to ooo how Dawson City inspired literary titans like Jack London and Robert Service – not just to write about the place but to live here too.

As for striking it lucky, your best chance is at Diamond Tooth Gertie's Gambling Hall, Canada's oldest legal casino, where women in breathtaking corsets and ruffle skirts hustle up drinks while you bet your way to boom or bust. Having doubled your chips at the roulette table, it's customary to celebrate

at the *Sourdough Saloon*, in the *Downtown Hotel*, where the house tipple is the sour-toe cocktail – a drink that includes a real pickled human toe in a shot of alcohol (local charitable frostbite victims keep the bar well-stocked). As the rule goes: you can drink it fast or drink it slow, but your lips must touch the toe.

NEED TO KNOW

You can reach Dawson City from Whitehorse by driving 536km along the North Klondike Hwy or by plane (1hr 15min 6 weekly; ⓦ www.flyairnorth.com). **Diamond Tooth Gertie's Gambling Hall** is at 4th Ave and Queen St (mid-May to mid-Sept daily 7pm–2am), the **Sourdough Saloon** is at 2nd Ave and Queen (☎ 867/993-5346).

reliving the wild west at the

Calgary
Stampede

10

Ten days each year, during the middle of July, the usually conservative city of Calgary loses its collective head (or finds a new cover for it, at least). Virtually everyone turns out in white Stetsons, bolo ties, blue jeans and hand-tooled boots, while addressing one another in bastardized cowboy slang. Rather than a new trend in fashion, it's a signal that it's time for the Calgary Stampede.

For Canada's rural folk – who often live on isolated farms or in tiny communities – this is the opportunity to bring their culture into the big city and really let rip. For the half-million visitors from elsewhere, it's a chance to witness the ultimate Wild West carnival, said to be North America's roughest rodeo.

Many activities, both kitschy and quite serious, vie for your attention. The main event is the daily rodeo competition, featuring the likes of bronco riding, native-buffalo riding, calf-roping, steer-wrestling, barrel-racing and wild-cow milking. But what sets the Stampede apart from other rodeos is the presence of the ludicrously dangerous, hugely exciting, chuck-wagon races: a team of

horsemen pack a stove and tent into a chuckwagon then rush around the track at breakneck speeds.

The non-rodeo action takes place at the festival's focal point, Stampede Park. Top attractions include a First Nations tepee village where you can try traditional foods; the satisfyingly obscure World Blacksmith Competition; and an Agricultural Building that's home to many a handsome cow and bull.

Finish each day with a dash of Stampede nightlife, yet another world unto itself. The drinking, gambling and partying at various bars and mega-cabarets goes on into the small hours, sustained by a seemingly endless supply of barbecued meat and baked beans.

NEED TO KNOW

Plan at least a year in advance for both accommodation and tickets for the annual Stampede. Tickets range from C$10 to C$50, and the upper stalls (J&K) are best for viewing the chuck-wagon races. For advance ticket sales and general information, visit ⓦ www.calgarystampede. com.

Eating
your way around the world in
Toronto

Walking around Toronto's main Chinatown, you may find resistance futile: the smells of spicy black bean sauce, Peking Duck and fried noodles hit you from every direction. Besides the restaurants – not all Chinese of course, with plenty of Vietnamese, Thai and Japanese eateries as well – street grocers vend everything from stinky durian fruit to delightful pork-stuffed buns. However, eating in Chinatown – like the rest of Toronto – is not just about the food: choose a restaurant busy with locals, order a cup of green or bubble tea, then sit back and be transported to the country of your choice.

Near Chinatown is Kensington Market, an ethnically diverse area crowded with street stalls. Dodge the clothing sellers and let your nose lead you to the food section, where you'll find a selection of crêpe and *poutine* vendors. A nod to early French and British influences, *poutine* is as close to a national dish as you'll get in a country this immense. Gloriously golden fries drip with melted cheese, capped by a pool of gravy; it's a simple pleasure that's actually quite hard to get right, as they do here.

The suburbs of Toronto also resemble hamlets of faraway lands. Little India is the

spot for your favourite spicy vindaloos and Little Portugal where to get a bowl of *caldo verde*, while in Greektown you'll find the perfect strong mid-afternoon cup of coffee alongside divine Greek pastries – a little pick-me-up before contemplating your next culinary stop.

For that, go back Downtown; while others line up for dinner at the rotating restaurant in the CN Tower, you might consider somewhere like *Canoe*, up on the 54th floor of the Dominion Tower. You still get great views, but in a less-touristy venue that happens to serve up some of the best Canadian food (and wines) in the country.

NEED TO KNOW

Chinatown and Kensington Market are both near Dundas Street West. The city's biggest food festival is the Taste of the Danforth in Greektown, held in the second weekend of August and showcasing food from more than sixty local restaurants (W www.tasteofthedanforth.com). **Canoe**, 66 Wellington St W (T 416/364-0054), offers tasting menus for around C$100; reservations are essential.

ski

from the sky in the

Rockies

The small town of Golden, between Glacier and Revelstoke national parks near the BC–Alberta border, doesn't seem like much passing through. But descend on a snowy peak in the area from a helicopter, skis in tow, and you're likely to form a totally different opinion.

Heliskiing got its start here, and the Rocky Mountains of British Columbia are still one of the best places on earth to do this terrifically expensive, fairly dangerous and undeniably thrilling activity. It's a pristine mountain wonderland filled with open bowls and endless tree runs, all coated in a layer of light and powdery snow. Accessing these stashes by helicopter, with its odd mix of mobility and avian fragility, only intensifies the feeling of exploration and isolation. From the air, you'll eagerly envision making your signature squiggles in the untouched powder fields. And once the helicopter leaves you alone and recedes into the distance, you'll feel every inch the pioneer.

After you've adjusted to the rhythm and bounce of skiing or riding this light powder, you might find yourself on a good day descending twice the typical distance as at a top ski resort.

You're also likely to discover that the deeper the snow and steeper the grade, the more exhilarating the run. Cornices and drop-offs that seemed foreboding from the helicopter will be a daring enticement; trees that from a distance looked impossibly dense reveal tempting paths; you'll drop into pitches that would have been unthinkable on harder snow, plunging in and out of chest-deep powder again and again. But be warned: all this may be enough to transform you into one of the many die-hards who sign up for their next heliskiing adventure the moment they reach base.

NEED TO KNOW

The heliskiing season runs from late-November to mid-May. Most heliski operations are concentrated in three major areas: the southern Rockies around Golden and Panorama; at the northern end of the range, just west of Jasper National Park; and further into British Columbia's interior around Revelstoke.

Costs and conditions vary: C$800 for a day, C$6000–7000 for a week, including accommodation and meals. Contact CMH Heli-Skiing (☏ 403/762-7100 or 1-800/661-0252, Ⓦ www.cmhski.com).

13 taking
afternoon tea in Victoria

Silver cutlery tinkles against Royal Doulton china as piano music wafts over idle chatter. "Would you like one lump or two?" inquires the waitress politely as she pours the piping hot tea. You'll take two, you say, and sink back into the floral sofa, taking in this most splendid view of Victoria's Inner Harbour from the *Tea Lobby* in the *Empress Hotel*. Rudyard Kipling once took afternoon tea in this very room and described Victoria as "Brighton Pavilion with the Himalayas for a backdrop". You can't help but agree with him.

Indeed, this provincial capital on the southern tip of wild and windy Vancouver Island is doing its bit to keep the 'British' in British Columbia. Vancouver may have embraced lofty glass condominiums and coffee, but across the Georgia Strait, Victoria has clung steadfastly to its English heritage, preserving its turn-of-the-twentieth-century architecture and keeping alive the age-old tradition of afternoon tea.

There are many quaint places in Victoria to indulge this whim – small suburban teahouses surrounded by royal family memorabilia, or amidst the floral finery of the Butchart Gardens – but none can match the palatial **Empress Hotel** for grandiosity or price. Shirley Temple, John Travolta and Queen Elizabeth II have all been spotted here piling on the pounds.

The multi-course ritual starts off innocently enough, with seasonal fruit topped with Chantilly cream along with a choice of eight tea blends. Then a three-tiered plate arrives, heaving with cucumber and smoked salmon sandwiches, raisin scones slathered with jam and clotted cream and, on top, a glorious selection of pastries oozing with chocolate. If you're too self-conscious to indulge in the very un-English practice of stuffing yourself silly, you could always fall back on the distinctly North American custom of asking for a doggie bag.

NEED TO KNOW

Afternoon tea at the **Empress Hotel**, 721 Government St (☎ 250/389-2727, 🌐 www .fairmont.com/empress) costs C$55 from June to August; reduced prices out of high season. Daily seatings start at noon.

Both a natural wonder and altogether otherworldly, the stunning aurora borealis (northern lights) are every bit worth travelling to the far reaches of Canada's Great North to see – and in subzero temperatures, no less. Some Inuit peoples believed they were the spirits of animals or ancestors, while others thought they represented wicked forces. Today, science explains the phenomenon as the result of "solar wind" – charged particles hurled from the sun and drawn into the earth's atmosphere by the magnetism of the poles – and the solar wind's interaction with the earth's magnetic field. Some of this energy is released as visible light, offering an extraordinary chance to observe the upper limits of the atmosphere.

The ethereal display can be seen over large areas of northern Canada, but nowhere better than during winter in Yellowknife, the capital of the Northwest Territories. Just 250 miles south of the Arctic Circle, Yellowknife's northerly location combined with the surrounding flat terrain offers the perfect vantage point.

A faint glow on the northeastern horizon after dusk signals that it's time to swaddle in parkas, ski pants, thick-soled boots, wooly headgear and gauntlet-sized gloves, and head out to watch the full show as night deepens. Eventually the sky will appear to shimmer with dancing curtains of colour, ranging from luminescent monotones – most commonly fantastic green or a dark red veil. Soon their movement becomes more animated, sometimes building up into a finale, in which rays seem to flare in all directions from a central point, slowly waving and swirling like incandescent tassels.

NEED TO KNOW

The lights are at their most dazzling between December and March, when the sun is out for only five hours a day and the temperature drops below -20°C/-4°F, though they're potentially visible all year round. The aurora borealis can't be predicted far in advance, but it is visible in Yellowknife about 296 nights per year; over a three-night stay you are virtually guaranteed to see them distinctly.

Find a forecast at ⊛www.gedds.alaska. edu/AuroraForecast. From Edmonton, First Air (☎613/839/3340, ⊛www .firstair.ca) flies half-cargo, half-passenger planes to Yellowknife.

viewing the

northern lights

lights

in Yellowknife

paddling your way through

Algonquin Provincial Park

The day may start like this: the rain eases and the mist on the lake begins to dissipate as the early sun breaks through the trees, onto your secluded campsite. You awaken to the melodious songs of warblers overhead, to the unspoiled wilderness of Algonquin Provincial Park.

After breakfast you put your canoe in the water and ponder your route. This dense, forested park has an extensive network of interconnected lakes, rivers and overland portages, some 1500km of paddling circuits; exploring by canoe is almost essential to understanding Algonquin. As you slide along you begin to get a truer sense of the dramatic landscape: thick stands of maples, towering red pines, black spruce bogs. There are granite ridges and sandy beaches and everywhere there is water, from ephemeral ponds to bottomless lakes.

You make chance acquaintances with wildlife. The canoe drifts by a lone moose foraging chest-deep in a marshy wetland; a black bear appears along the shore – the distance between the two of you feels close enough. A beaver quietly constructs his lodge in a transparent pond, and a family of newly emerged mergansers swims alongside your small craft, like nonpaying passengers on your voyage.

At the end of a long day's paddle the blue skies give way to a star-filled night and you settle around the crackling campfire to a plate of freshly caught fish. A new cast of characters croon their forest tunes: the haunted calls of loons ricochet off the lakeshores, wolves howl in distant highlands. A barred owl hoots, and you think you might be hearing things. In a place where you could easily go for days on end without human contact, you may swear it said, "Who cooks for you? Who cooks for you all?"

NEED TO KNOW

Algonquin Provincial Park (Ⓦ www. algonquin.on.ca) begins about 250km north of Toronto. Various outfitters renting canoes and camping supplies can be found along the Parkway Corridor (Highway 60). Camping fees are around C$9 per night and advance bookings are recommended – try ⓣ 1-888/668-7275 or Ⓦ www.camis.com/op/default. asp. Alternatively, several tour operators offer all-inclusive fully guided canoe trips through the park, which will run about C$400 for a long weekend.

Saturday is known, on TV at least, as "Hockey Night in Canada" – pretty much all you need to know in terms of the country's fanaticism for its national game. Actually, lacrosse is the official national game, but it doesn't arouse nearly the same passions.

Perhaps it's the nature of the game itself. You'll have to focus hard to track the movement of the puck and the hurried but fluid way the teams shift players – frequently – in the middle of it all. And with those skaters hurtling around at 50kph and pucks clocking speeds above 160kph, this would

be a high-adrenaline sport even without its relaxed attitude to combat on the rink – as an old Canadian adage has it, "I went to see a fight and an ice-hockey game broke out".

To maximize your exposure to the madness, get a seat near the rink for a game matching old rivals. Any of the six Canada-based teams will do, but when the Montréal Canadiens, the most successful team in hockey history, and the Toronto Maple Leafs, part of the National Hockey League since 1927, meet – mirroring the the country's Francophone

and Anglophone divisions – you'll get a real feel for the electricity a match can generate. You may even see a hockey game break out.

NEED TO KNOW

Tickets, which start from about C$20, need to be bought in advance for nearly all matches; check the club websites for info via links at ⊛ www.nhl.com. The Canadiens play at the **Molson Centre**, 1260, rue de la Gauchetière Ouest, Montréal (☎1-800/361-4595), while the Maple Leafs play at the **Air Canada Centre**, 40 Bay St, Toronto (☎416/815-5500).

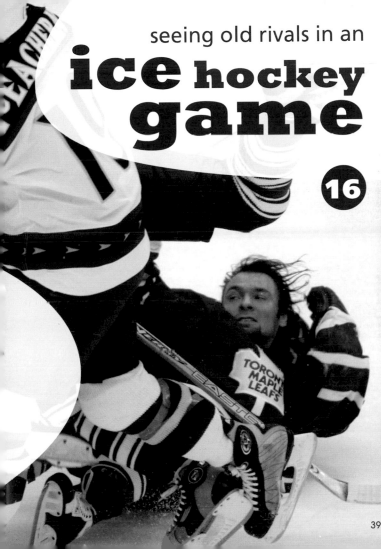

seeing old rivals in an

ice hockey game

16

"This wondertrail will be world renowned", predicted a 1920s surveyor when Highway 93 North – now better known as the Icefields Parkway – was only a fanciful idea. And sure enough, when it opened twenty years later, built as a Depression-era public works program, the 230-kilometre road between Lake Louise and Jasper immediately became one of the world's ultimate drives.

It still is. The highway snakes through the cornucopia of snow-capped peaks that crown the Continental Divide, running right down the heart of the Rockies. Between the peaks lies an almost overwhelming combination of natural splendour: immense glaciers, blue-green iridescent lakes, foaming waterfalls, wildflower meadows, forests and wildlife from elk and moose to brown bears and grizzly bears.

You could drive the whole highway in about four hours, but to do so would be to miss out on the many trails and viewpoints along the way, as well as the chance to properly appreciate all the subtle shifts in scenery and mood: rivers broaden or narrow, move from churning to sluggish; light changes according to the fickle mountain weather, sometimes producing a rosy pink reflection on a distant peak.

driving the

Icefields Parkway

Several points along the route outstrip any superlatives. Bow Pass, at 2070m the road's highest point, is spectacular not only for the views but the delicate sub-alpine ecosystem that ekes out its existence at these windy, snowy heights. Here moss-lined paths lead between dark stands of towering fir and spruce while mountain heather and alpine forget-me-nots provide splashes of pink, yellow and white.

Far bleaker is the 125-square-mile Columbia Icefield itself – one of the largest accumulations of ice south of the Arctic Circle. Its rock-strewn moonscape has remained virtually unchanged since the last ice age, and at its edge you can watch 200-year-old snow slowly melting.

NEED TO KNOW

Car rental outlets abound in Banff and Jasper, but if you'd rather someone else do the driving – and give you background along the way – take a trip with **Brewster Vacations** (around C$400; ☎ 403/762-6717, or 1-800/661-1152, Ⓦ www.brewster.ca). The tour includes a ride on an Ice Explorer – an all-terrain vehicle with tires five feet in diameter – on the Columbia Icefield and a night's stay in a Jasper hotel.

Haida Gwaii

18

Soaking in natural hot springs on a rainforest island while a pod of humpback whales swim past . . . suddenly the "Canadian Galápagos" moniker occasionally used to describe the remote archipelago of Haida Gwaii doesn't seem so far-fetched.

Cast some 150km off the west coast of British Columbia, Haida Gwaii (formerly the Queen Charlotte Islands) is a place where the world's largest black bears forage on deserted beaches, black-footed albatross show off their enormous wingspan, and sea stars the size of coffee tables and the shades of disco lights sprawl languidly on rocks.

Only two thousand people a year make the journey to the pristine national park in the southern portion of the islands. Here, it takes eight people to hug a thousand-year-old cedar

tree, months to kayak around the 1750km of coastline, and a lifetime to fully comprehend the 10,000-year-old civilization that once inhabited the islands.

There is an underlying eeriness to this place that was, until recently, home to thousands of Haida – the most sophisticated and artistically prolific of British Columbia's indigenous people.

These days, moss-covered beams of long houses and decaying totem poles are the lingering remains of the ancient Haida villages, whose populations left after being drastically reduced in an 1880s smallpox epidemic. The most haunting and remote of the deserted villages is SGang Gwaay (Ninstints), a mist-shrouded UNESCO World Heritage Site on the southernmost tip of the park, where the world's

largest collection of Haida mortuary poles stare defiantly out to sea.

Looking up at this forest of tree trunks – expertly carved with the wide-eyed features of bears, frogs, beavers, eagles, ravens and whales – is to gaze into the weather-beaten face of history. However, as is the wish of the Haida, there is little attempt at preserving the totems. Some day soon the poles will lean, fall, rot, and – like everything else here – return to nature.

NEED TO KNOW

Haida Gwaii can be reached by ferry (six hours) or seaplane (one hour) from Prince Rupert, or by plane from Vancouver (two hours). For information on travelling to **Gwaii Haanas National Park Reserve and Haida Heritage Site** call ☏ 250/559-8818 or see ⓦ www.pc.gc.ca /gwaiihaanas.

The Prarie provinces of Saskatchewan and Manitoba have a somewhat unfair reputation for being uninspiring and dreary. There's no denying the winters are bitingly cold – temperatures regularly sit below -40°C/-40°F and residents of Winnipeg have been known to break out the shorts when it climbs to 10°C/14°F – and perhaps the area lacks any dynamic must-see cities. But the Prairies are also

the heartland of Canada, a wide-open landscape untainted by glittering skyscrapers and traffic congestion, seen to best advantage on a coast-to-coast train ride.

The train originates in Vancouver, but it's not until it heads east from Edmonton that the Prairie landscape begins. From there a blanket of darkness, decorated only by stars, engulfs you. When the train

pulls into Saskatchewan's capital, Saskatoon, around 2am, you're fast asleep, lulled by the train's movement, surrounded by the same darkened sky and glistening stars.

Rise in the morning and head to the viewing dome car for a panoramic view of the countryside. Snow-capped mountains and towering trees are a distant memory, replaced by seemingly endless fields of

crossing the

Prairies by

train

wheat and grassland. There are no houses, no signs of life except for the occasional view of elk or deer grazing trackside.

The hypnotic monotony of the journey is broken by a brief stop in Winnipeg. Canada's coldest city, "Winterpeg" is home to the windiest intersection in the country and a heated labyrinth weaving its way under the central shopping arcade. Leaving the city,

you see proof of population – grain elevators and wheat silos dot the horizon, most approaching ruin; battered by the elements, they now provide a perch for the large number of bird species who feed off the fields of grain.

When you finally step off the train at its ultimate destination, bustling Toronto, the serenity of the Prairies becomes a distant, lovely memory.

NEED TO KNOW

The journey from Vancouver to Toronto (you can also do it in reverse) straight through takes three days: **VIA Rail** trains (☎ 1-888/842 7245, Ⓦ www.viarail.ca) depart from Vancouver on Tuesday, Friday and Sunday at 5.30pm and a one-way ticket costs from C$450. You could also purchase a Canrail pass entitling you to twelve days travel in a 30-day period, allowing you to hop on and off at will.

coasting on the

P'tit Train
du Nord

After a day of pedalling, a long downhill coast is a moment to be savoured. On either side the forest is a blur of green tinged with gold and the breeze ruffling your hair smells faintly of pine and earth. The treetops almost form a tunnel around the trail but in the glimpses of sky loom crinkled mountains, and off to the right, screened by foliage, roars the frothing fury of the Rivière Rouge, the Red River.

In the silence of the forest it's hard to imagine that fume-belching locomotives once thundered along the same route as your bicycle tires. The P'tit Train du Nord was a busy railroad for eighty years, eventually closing in 1989. Instead of abandoning the route to the forest, the rail bed was transformed into a magnificent cycle trail that winds for 200km through the splendour of the Laurentian region of southwest Québec. Many of the original railroad station houses have been converted into cafés, information booths and facilities for cyclists, their decorative wooden gables and shady terraces restored with vibrant paint and blooming baskets.

The northern half of the trail is wild and remote, crossing numerous rivers died chestnut-brown by minerals and passing blue-black lakes close enough to wet your wheels. Small villages full of silver-steepled churches and impossibly cozy cottages cluster around the southern half of the trail. But whichever part you choose to ride (if not the whole course), nearly every bend holds an inviting picnic spot to laze in or a shady pool to revive sore feet and aching muscles.

NEED TO KNOW

The two-hundred-kilometre P'Tit Train du Nord typically takes 3 to 4 days, starting in Saint-Jérôme and ending in Mont-Laurier. There are plenty of service points and accommodation along the entire trail. You can choose to take panniers and camp or cycle from inn to inn and have your luggage transported (ⓦ www.transportduparclineaire.com). A daily trail pass is C$5, or C$15 for the season (May to October).

spying
whales
and spotting
puffins

in Newfoundland

Every spring and summer the waters off the coasts of Newfoundland and Labrador play host to the largest concentration of nesting seabirds and migrating humpback whales anywhere in the world. This spectacle unfolds just a few kilometres off shore, at the confluence of the warm Gulf Stream and the frigid Labrador Current. Here, where cod has been overfished to the point of near-elimination, nature enthusiasts come to experience the thrill of seeing hundreds of thousands of nesting seabirds, the feeding frenzy of 40-tonne whales and the occasional sighting of a 10,000 year-old iceberg drifting southwards from its Arctic home.

The way to observe this is on board one of the many passenger ferries that operate from Bay Bulls Harbour, bound for the Witless Bay Ecological Reserve. As your boat chugs towards the mist-shrouded islands the patter of your guides and the jovial folk singing recede in deference to a loud hum, accompanied by an overpowering stench – its origin only apparent when the fog lifts. All of a sudden you're surrounded by what seems like millions of clown-faced puffins, penguin-like murres and black-legged kittiwakes diving in and out of the waters, delivering beakloads of capelin to their young.

The flurry of activity overhead nearly distracts you from seeing the tell-tale spray of a giant humpback in the distance. A short while later a guide announces that a small pod of minke whales have been spotted near the stern. Soon more dorsal fins slice through the gentle swells and the characteristic forked tails slap the seas as the whales submerge to feed. It's only now that you appreciate the immense size of these cetaceans as they follow alongside your boat.

The three-hour cruise is over far too quickly. Before you know it your guide asks, "Are you ready to become an honorary Newfoundlander?" Your intentions seem obvious as you quickly down a shot of Screech (the local rum) and kiss a stuffed puffin in front of a rowdy group of fellow passengers.

NEED TO KNOW

There are several tour operators in Bay Bulls Harbour, a 30min drive south of the St John's. The best time for spotting whales and icebergs is late spring and early summer. **Gatherall's Puffin and Whale Watch Tours** offers numerous daily tours to the Witless Bay Ecological Reserve (ⓦ www. gatheralls.com). Prices start at C$49 per adult.

Head-Smashed-in Buffalo Jump

22

Long ago, our ancestors subsisted on berries, roots, birds and small animals. Buffalo herds roamed the grasslands of the Great Plains, but they weren't hunted, as these enormous, horned mammals attacked humans. Then one day as Napi, the Blackfoot Supreme Being, visited his people, he saw scattered bodies that had been partly devoured by buffalo. Napi declared, "This will not do, I will change this. My people shall eat the buffalo".

This was one of several stories told to us by our host, a young member of the Blackfoot's Peigan tribe, around the campfire of the tipi site beneath poetically named Head-Smashed-In Buffalo Jump. Here, in southern Alberta, Napi supposedly led a buffalo herd to the rugged Porcupine Hills and unveiled the pis'kun – buffalo jump – method of killing the animal. Whatever credence the myth has, Head-Smashed-In was used as a staging ground for killing great numbers of bison for over 10,000 years, up until around 150 years ago.

Earlier that day, our host had shown us V-shaped lanes along which buffalo, stalked by hundreds of Blackfoot braves

wrapped in buffalo or coyote robes, were stampeded in a tight herd, led over the dust-obscured cliff to fall to their deaths. Cunningly built into the cliff now is an impressive interpretive centre, which further explains the custom and offers excellent insight into the old Blackfoot way of life. But so did our guide, who stressed how the Blackfoot let nothing go to waste. Objects fashioned from a bewildering array of buffalo parts got passed around; for the Blackfoot, a herd resembled "a walking department store", providing for their every need.

In this remote provincial corner, the beast remains a powerful cultural symbol, and a night's camping the chance to commune with a disappearing way of life.

As midnight struck and the fire burned its last, we entered our tipi. The moon and stars illuminated the vast prairie, the still night interrupted only by the occasional mooing of cattle grazing on the range beyond the campsite.

NEED TO KNOW

Head-Smashed-In, a World Heritage Site, is 18km northwest of Fort Macleod and 180km south of Calgary. Camping programmes run from mid-May to mid-Sept and cost C$320 for a group of four or fewer.

Advance reservations are essential; check Ⓦ www.head-smashed-in.com or call ☎ 403-553-2731.

There's an eerieness to the Bay of Fundy, never more so than when the banking fogs that sweep in off the Atlantic shroud its churning waters, rendering its sea cliffs and coves barely visible in an all-pervasive gloom. Tourist brochures would lovingly call this "atmospheric", which it is. But what they tend to play up more are the bay's impressive stats: this is where the highest tides in the world come crashing in – there up to 16m difference between high tide and low tide; in some places, the tide retreats 4 to 5km (2.5 to 3 miles) as it ebbs.

You don't need numbers, just your own eyes. Stand on the steps at Evangeline Beach in Grand-Pré, and see young boys peddling bicycles across far-reaching mud flats, then return a few hours later to find the beach deserted, the water ten feet high and rising. You could build a giant IMAX movie screen on the mud flats at low tide and it would be completely submerged at high tide, just six hours later.

The effect comes in part from the bay's shape. At its mouth it is 100km wide, but it gradually narrows and shallows, producing

watching the tide roll away in
the Bay of Fundy

a funnelling effect when the water comes in. Many of the rivers that lead off the upper bay are sites of tidal bores – basically the name for what occurs when the water rushes against the current. This is what people come to see.

When you first spot it from a distance, it may be subtle: just a faint line across a wide section of water. But as the river narrows and the water closes in, seeming to pick up speed, it's more like a moving wall – one that submerges islets, rides up high on floating docks and provides plenty of challenge for those fool enough to break out surfboards or inflatable Zodiac boats.

NEED TO KNOW

Separating Nova Scotia from New Brunswick, the Bay of Fundy is 290km long and between 120 and 215m deep. Allow about two hours for the drive north from Halifax, Nova Scotia, to the eastern reaches of the Bay of Fundy, a little longer if you're driving south from Fredericton, the capital of New Brunswick. Truro, Moncton and Saint John are good bases for trying to see a tidal bore.

staying afloat on

Little Manitou Lake

In the minds of most Canadians, Saskatchewan is the heart of the rather plain Prairies: a land of vast skies and dull Trans-Canada Highway drives. But within easy reach of the highway lies a lake with world-class therapeutic waters that must rank as the province's, if not the country's, best-kept secret. Little Manitou Lake and the adjacent basic Manitou Springs resort offer a no-frills spa experience where you come out heavily coated with minerals and feeling much the better for it.

Reasons to soak here go well beyond skin therapy, the relief of aches and pains, or even the many claimed cures attributed to the waters: in short, it's just a whole lot of fun. With the water three times saltier than seawater and denser than that of the Dead Sea, you'll find yourself floating on the surface, feet up. This unique sensation of floating effortlessly is as close as you'll likely get to the weightlessness of space; it brings with it all sorts of acrobatic possibilities, or just the chance to bob on your back and comfortably read a newspaper.

The waters have long been celebrated, first by the Native Americans who camped on its shored and named it for its healing properties, later by homesteaders who spread the news of the mineral-rich lake and of course by the Manitou Mineral Water Company, which shipped it as a product all across North America. But things have quieted down from its heights as a spa town, so for once, there are few to rebuke you for time spent aimlessly adrift.

NEED TO KNOW

Little Manitou Lake lies beside the small town of Watrous, some 116km southeast of Saskatoon and 185km north of Regina. Adjacent to the lake, the basic full-service **Manitou Springs hotel** (☎ 306/946-2233 or 1-800-667-7672, ⓦ www.manitousprings.ca; double rooms cost around C$120) is a convenient choice, since use of the golden brown mineral waters in its pool – pumped in from Little Manitou and heated – is included in rates. Otherwise a dip costs C$10. The hotel and pools are open year-round.

catching a wave on
Vancouver Island

For some of the wildest surfing in the world, head to the shipwreck-strewn west coast of Vancouver Island, also known as "the graveyard of the Pacific". Flanked by the lush temperate rainforest of the 130 kilometre-long Pacific Rim National Park, the waters here are ferocious. Swells reach up to six metres, and epic storms uproot trees, sending drifting logs down the face of waves. Whales have been known to sneak up on unsuspecting surfers, diving under their boards and lifting them clean out of the water. And barking territorial sea lions will chase surfers from the ocean back to shore. On land, it's just as wild – bald eagles soar between giant trees, and wolves and black bears fossick for food amid piles of sun-bleached driftwood.

Even in summer, when swells ease to a gentle one to two metres, the water remains bone-chillingly cold, hovering around 13°C/55°F. Plenty of wannabe surfies flock to the chilled-out surf centre of Tofino to practise their "pop-ups", but a thick skin – or a thick wetsuit – is required.

Come winter, the waves start pummelling in from the Pacific like a boxer laying a victory blow. The wind whips off the snow-capped mountains, the ocean cools down to a shocking 8°C/46°F and hardy surfers hit the waves wearing five-millimetre-thick wetsuits as well as boots, gloves and protective hoods.

For the novice, it's time to peel off the wetsuit and watch the waves roll in from the blissful confines of a seaside hot tub.

NEED TO KNOW

Tofino is on the west coast of Vancouver Island; see ⓦ www.tourismtofino.com for information. **Westside Surf School** (☎ 250-725-2404, ⓦ www. westsidesurfschool) and **Surf Sister Surf School** (☎ 250/725-4456, ⓦ www.surfsister .com) offer two-hour lessons on Long Beach for C$75.

25

Ultimate
experiences
Canada
miscellany

1 People

Canada has 33 million people, of whom some 86% are white. Around 10% are Asian, with a third of those ethnically Chinese; 2% are black, mostly from the Caribbean; and around 3% are native or aboriginal peoples, speaking some fifty different languages.

2 Five great Canadian movies

The Barbarian Invasions (2003). Québec's leading director Denys Arcand applies his signature style of dialogue-heavy realism to Montréal intellectuals and their politics, sexuality and mortality.

Exotica (1994). Perhaps the most existential film ever set in a strip club (in Toronto), imagined by Atom Egoyan in dramatic and eye-opening detail.

Mon Oncle Antoine (1972). Claude Jutra's bracing, realist classic of a young boy growing up in a mining town in Québec still resonates after more than thirty years.

Neighbours (1952). Norman McLaren did pioneering work for the National Film Board of Canada, but may be most known for this short, scathing satire about two men going to war over possession of a flower.

Videodrome (1983). Still one of the creepiest films ever, David Cronenberg's opus filmed in Toronto has much in common with the rest of his work – sex, obsession, decay, violence and an odd sort of humour.

3 Prime ministers

There have been 22 Canadian prime ministers in 140 years, starting with Sir John A. Macdonald in 1867 and leading up to Stephen Harper today. Perhaps the most dominant recent PM was **Pierre Trudeau**, who, except for one year in 1979–1980, led the Liberal majority in Parliament from 1968 to 1984.

The prime minister, of course, is not the official head of state – that crown belongs to the **reigning monarch of the United Kingdom**. Although Elizabeth II has been Canada's head of state since 1952, the country has had only one woman prime minister – Kim Campbell, who served just over four months in 1993.

4 Cities, provinces and territories

Canada comprises ten provinces, which have some autonomy within the federation, and three territories, which are more dependent on the federal government and have only one-third of one percent of the country's people.

Province/territory	% of Canadian population	Capital	Largest city
Ontario	38	Toronto	Toronto
Québec	23	Québec City	Montréal
British Columbia	13	Victoria	Vancouver
Alberta	10	Calgary	Edmonton
Manitoba	3.6	Winnipeg	Winnipeg
Saskatchewan	3	Regina	Saskatoon
Nova Scotia	3	Halifax	Halifax
New Brunswick	2	Fredericton	Saint John
Newfoundland and Labrador	1.5	St John's	St John's
Prince Edward Island	1	Charlottetown	Charlottetown
Northwest Territories	<1	Yellowknife	Yellowknife
Yukon	<1	Whitehorse	Whitehorse
Nunavut	<1	Iqaluit	Iqaluit

The biggest cities are, in order, Toronto, Montréal, Vancouver, Ottawa, Calgary and Edmonton. Toronto is also the fifth-biggest city in North America, its 2.6 million residents putting it just behind Chicago.

"A Canadian is sort of like an American, but without the gun.

Anonymous

5 Five unusual hotels

Chateau Montebello, Montebello, Québec. Once known as the world's largest log cabin, this classic 1930s resort still has a rough-hewn charm amid the modern luxury.

Fantasy Land, Edmonton, Alberta. The ultimate in kid-friendly theme accommodation, with the rooms decked out in 120 different styles, from ancient Roman to Polynesian.

Ice Hotel, Québec City, Québec. Constructed entirely of ice, this deep-frozen luxury item is only open three months of the year, so book a igloo-style room before the place melts.

Sentry Mountain Lodge, Golden, British Columbia. Poised at 7000ft on a snowy peak, this elegant retreat is only accessible by helicopter.

West Point Lighthouse, O'Leary, Prince Edward Island. Rugged 1875 lighthouse tower that holds a romantic, windswept B&B.

6 Rocks and lakes

Canada is built on some of the oldest rocks in the world. The **Canadian Shield**, a huge swath of terrain roughly stretching around Hudson Bay, is made up of a good amount of Precambrian metamorphic rock, some of it 4.5 billion years – or as old as the earth itself.

Most of Canada's **lakes** derive from the effects of the Ice Age, when huge retreating **glaciers** cut deep crevasses across the landscape or, in the case of the largest, Hudson Bay, depressed the land enough to allow it to fill with water. Not counting the Great Lakes (of which Superior and Huron would be the nation's biggest), the largest lakes fully within Canada are: **Great Bear**, Northwest Territories (31,328 sq km)

Great Slave, Northwest Territories (28,568 sq km)

Winnipeg, Manitoba (24,400 sq km)

Athabasca, Alberta/Saskatchewan (7935 sq km)

Reindeer, Saskatchewan/Manitoba (6650 sq km)

I don't even know what street Canada is on.
Al Capone

7 SCTV

The groundbreaking comedy troupe Second City started in the 1970s and led to its own late-night television show, SCTV, first syndicated and later on NBC. It showcased a wide array of performers, some of whom would later appear in TV shows like **Saturday Night Live** and movies such as **Strange Brew, Waiting for Guffman** and **Best in Show**. Cast members included:

Comedian	Typical character	Most famous character
John Candy	jovial fat man	Yosh Schmenge
Joe Flaherty	neurotic bigshot	Guy Caballero
Eugene Levy	sleazy nerd	Bobby Bittman
Andrea Martin	annoying eccentric	Edith Prickley
Rick Moranis	antic short fellow	Bob Mackenzie
Catherine O'Hara	ditzy blonde	Lola Heatherton
Harold Ramis	sneaky oddball	Moe Green
Martin Short	excitable freak	Ed Grimley
Dave Thomas	suspicious lunkhead	Doug Mackenzie

8 Tall buildings

Canada boasts the tallest freestanding structure in the world, the CN Tower (553m). It's in Toronto, as are the country's five tallest buildings:

Building	Height	Storeys	Built in
First Canadian Place	298m	72	1975
Scotia Plaza	275m	68	1988
TD Canada Trust Tower	261m	53	1990
Commerce Court	239m	57	1972
Toronto-Dominion Centre	239m	56	1967

9 French Canada

By the mid-eighteenth-century France controlled a huge swath of territory from what's now Canada down to the Mississippi River and Gulf Coast to the Caribbean. That reign ended with the country's loss in the Seven Years War to Britain in 1763.

Although Britain expelled the **Acadians** of Nova Scotia (to Louisiana, where they became "Cajuns"), most French speakers remained, and today form a **Francophone belt** that includes all of Québec and parts of Ontario and New Brunswick.

Québec is Canada's only **majority-French-speaking province**, where 82% of the population speaks the language – more than six times the amount of English speakers.

"Canadians have been so busy explaining to the Americans that we aren't British, and to the British that we aren't Americans that we haven't had time to become Canadians."

Helen Gordon McPherson

10 War

The land that would become Canada saw countless conflicts between Britain, France, the United States and native peoples over the centuries. Since 1867, the modern country has been involved in **seven major wars**, usually at the behest of Britain or the United States:

North-West Rebellion (1885)
Second Boer War (1899–1902)
World War I (1914–18)
World War II (1939–45)
Korean War (1951–53)
Persian Gulf War (1991)
Afghanistan Invasion (2001)

 **Rivers**

Canada's rivers empty into three different oceans – Atlantic, Pacific, and Arctic – as well as Hudson Bay and even the Gulf of Mexico. The **longest** that flow mostly through the country are:

Mackenzie (4241km)
St Lawrence (3058km)
Nelson (2575km)
Churchill (1609km)
Fraser (1370km)

 Music

▶▶ Ten great albums by Canadians

Music from Big Pink (1968) by The Band. Folk-flavoured roots rock that turned the flower-power era on its ear, with some help from Bob Dylan.

Songs of Leonard Cohen (1968) by Leonard Cohen. Gloomy introspection and a true poetic flair are the hallmarks of this legendary troubadour.

After the Gold Rush (1970) by Neil Young. A lovely song cycle that defined his early blend of folk and hippie rock.

American Woman (1970) by the Guess Who. The incendiary title track is a signature moment in Canadian–American relations.

Blue (1971) by Joni Mitchell. If "A Case of You" doesn't bring shivers to your spine, there may be no hope.

Moving Pictures (1981) by Rush. Hoary rockers at their commercial and critical peak – "Tom Sawyer" still sounds fresh after 25 years.

The Trinity Sessions (1988) by Cowboy Junkies. Spare, sultry music perfect for late-night listening.

When I Was a Boy (1993) by Jane Siberry. With some help from Brian Eno, an underrated songstress finds her surest footing.

Poses (2002) by Rufus Wainwright. Slightly cheating (he's half-Canadian and did grow up in Montréal), but pop music this shimmering and soulful deserves every plug possible.

Funeral (2004) by Arcade Fire. The brightest current hope for Canadian rock – with a huge cast of musicians and a cache of infectious melodies.

13 Cheese fries and Chinese pies

Not surprisingly, Canadian cuisine ranges widely, from the heavily French-influenced fare of Québec to the seafood of the coastal provinces to the Western-style steaks and hearty eats of the prairie and Rocky Mountain region.

Signature dish	Region	What it is
Bannock	eastern	Scottish-derived flat oatmeal cake
Beaver tails	Ontario	flavoured fried dough
Butter tart	general	small sugar pie
Donair	general	meat and sauce rolled in a pita
Fiddleheads	New Brunswick	cooked young ferns
Nanaimo bar	British Columbia	custard-and-chocolate bar
Oreilles de Christ	Québec	"Ears of Christ", deep-fried pork jowls
Paté chinois	Québec	"Chinese pie". with corn, beef and mashed potatoes
Pemmican	western	native beef jerky with berries
Poutine	Québec	French fries with cheese curds and gravy
Tourtiere	Québec	meat pie stuffed with pork, veal or beef
Xoosum	British Columbia	native-style ice cream

"In any world menu, Canada must be considered the vichyssoise of nations – it's cold, half-French, and difficult to stir."

Stuart Keate

14 Provincial mottos

Alberta	Strong and free
British Columbia	Splendour without diminishment
Manitoba	Glorious and free
New Brunswick	Hope was restored
Newfoundland	Seek ye first the kingdom of God
Nova Scotia	One defends and the other conquers
Nunavut Territory	Our land, our strength
Ontario	Loyal she began, loyal she remains
Prince Edward Island	The strong under the protection of the great
Québec	I remember
Saskatchewan	From many peoples, strength

15 Political parties

Canadian politics is based on a **parliamentary system**. Though virtually any party can be represented in Parliament, some run strictly on a regional basis, such as the Bloc Québécois.

Party	Established	Politics
Bloc Québecois	1993	socialist, Québec separatist
Conservative	2003	economically and socially conservative, western-provincial orientation
Green	1983	environmental, leftist
Liberal	1867	liberal, progressive, strong in Ontario
Libertarian	1975	economically conservative, socially moderate
New Democratic	1961	populist/socialist
Progressive Canadian	2004	economically and socially moderate, splinter from the Conservative party

 16 Religion

Canadians affiliated by religion are 77% Christian, 2% Muslim, and 1% each Buddhist, Hindu, Sikh, and Jewish, while 17% claim no affiliation. The largest denominations are Catholic (43%), Protestant (29%), and Eastern Orthodox (2%). Half of all Catholics reside in Québec (which is 83% Catholic).

The largest and most eye-catching **churches** and **cathedrals** also tend to be in Québec, though a few others are sprinkled elsewhere:

Cathedral or church	Location	Year built	Features
Notre-Dame de Québec	Québec City	1786–1822	Neoclassical, among the oldest parishes in North America
Notre-Dame de Montréal	Montréal	1830	Gothic Revival icon, perhaps the most beautiful in Canada
St James	Toronto	1844	English Gothic, with a 93m-tall spire
St John the Baptist	St John's	1855	Romanesque Revival, once the largest in North America
St Joseph's Oratory	Montréal	1917–67	Renaissance Revival, largest church in Canada, second-largest dome in the world

17 Ten great works of Canadian fiction

The Handmaid's Tale by Margaret Atwood. Terrifying tale of a misogynist dystopia, rendered with the same dark colours as Orwell's 1984.

The Deptford Trilogy by Robertson Davies. Davies memorably spins picaresque tales of mystery and magic in the early twentieth century.

Neuromancer by William Gibson. The propulsive, futuristic work that jump-started the cyberpunk craze.

A Stone Angel by Margaret Laurence. Set in a fictional Manitoban town, this moving book champions female independence in the 1960s.

Pelagie: The Return to Acadie by Antonine Maillet. Inspired by Homer's *Ulysses*, a sweeping narrative of exile and adventure set in the world of British-controlled Acadia.

The Love of a Good Woman by Alice Munro. A selection by Canada's most renowned short-story author, mainly set in the West.

Black Robe by Brian Moore. *Lonely Passion of Judith Hearne* may be better known, but it's set in Belfast, unlike this story of a missionary in 1600s Québec.

The English Patient by Michael Ondaatje. Complex, multilayered narrative of love, loss, and mystery at the end of World War II. Much better than the Hollywood version.

The Apprenticeship of Duddy Kravitz by Mordecai Richler. Early novel by the comic master, detailing the obsessive rise of a young man out of working-class Montréal.

The Tin Flute by Gabrielle Roy. Groundbreaking French-language story of the Depression's effect on the poor of Montréal.

18 Far and wide

The second biggest country in the world, Canada is huge: almost 10 million sq km in area, with a top distance of 5700km between the edges of Newfoundland and the Yukon Territory – or the same distance from Toronto to London. The most extreme points of all are:

Point	Name	Location	Feature
northernmost	Cape Columbia	Ellesmere Island, Nunavut	world's northernmost after Greenland
southernmost	Middle Island	near Pelee Island, Ontario	bird sanctuary
westernmost	Beaver Creek	western Yukon Territory	Alaska border town
easternmost	Cape Spear	near St John's, Newfoundland	lighthouse site

"It's going to be a great country when they finish unpacking it".

Andrew H. Malcolm

19 Popular culture

Perhaps because of their ability to encounter mass (American) society while also standing apart from it, Canadian thinkers have in the last several decades been some of the keenest observers of the Western zeitgeist. Notable ideas and trends to emerge include:

Cyberpunk Vancouver resident William Gibson inaugurated the postmodern sci-fi movement with his novel *Neuromancer*, detailing a high-tech world of artificial intelligence, drugs, computers, and laissez-faire capitalism.

The Medium Is the Message Our era's most important theorist, Marshall McLuhan posited that the presence of any medium – TV, movies, radio – is more important than its content in its cultural impact.

The Global Village Another McLuhan idea that was decades ahead of its time, predicting the effects of an interlinked world on economies, nations, values, and consciousness – as well as human freedom, tyranny and terror.

Generation X Taken from a British punk band, novelist Douglas Coupland's moniker for the supposedly cynical and aimless successor to the Me Generation gained traction in the 1990s.

20 Where the buffalo roam
▶▶ Distinctive Canadian wildlife

Bald eagles formidable bird of prey found across most of Canada.

Bears grizzly, black, brown, and polar bears roam the West and North.

Bighorn sheep their signature curved horns are seen across the Mountain West.

Bison nearly driven to extinction; spotted in zoological parks.

Blue herons stately water birds known for lunging at and catching fish.

Canada geese long-necked birds, seen in flocks across the continent.

Caribou and elk with great antlers and stealthy speed, a majestic species in the West.

Cougars typically spotted at night in the wooded Rockies.

Moose colossal members of the deer family, found across Canada's southern tier.

Mountain goats a familiar presence perched on the cliffs of the Rockies.

Whales orcas to humpbacks, minke and beluga swim in coastal waters.

Wolves target for hunters, but still a vibrant species living in packs up North.

 **Canadian art**

Museum	Location	Strengths
Art Gallery of Toronto	Toronto	international modern art
Museum of Fine Arts	Montréal	Canadian, European, decorative
National Gallery of Canada	Ottawa	international Modern art
Royal Ontario Museum	Toronto	international. art, human and natural history
Vancouver Art Gallery	Vancouver	modern art, Chagall, Emily Carr

 **Sport**

Canadians play most of the same sports their American counterparts do, with a few exceptions; the following arguably get the most attention:

Bowling Played on lawns or alleys; Canada has its own unique "five-pin" variant.

Curling Shuffleboard on ice, this game is huge in the prairie West.

Football, Association The world's essential game.

Football, Canadian More wide-open variation of US football, played on a bigger field.

Hockey Played on every level, with six major-league teams.

Lacrosse Popular summer sport.

Rugby Club sport for nearly 150 years, now big on national level.

"Canada is a country whose main exports are hockey players and cold fronts. Our main imports are baseball players and acid rain."
Pierre Trudeau

23 Rocky Mountain high?

Most of Canada's tallest mountains are near Alaska in the Yukon Territory, where you can find all of the top ten, except for Fairweather in British Columbia; surprisingly, none is in the area known for its mountains, the Canadian Rockies, which stretches between Alberta and British Columbia.

Logan (5950m)

St Elias (5490m)

Lucania (5230m)

King Peak (5170m)

Steele (5070m)

Wood (4840m)

Vancouver (4790m)

Slaggard (4740m)

MacAuley (4700m)

Fairweather (4670m)

24 Native peoples

The native peoples of Canada number less than a million, and have been categorized in three distinct groups: the **Metis**, largely in the western provinces, whose mixed heritage derives from aboriginal peoples and British and French-Canadian settlers; the **Inuit**, formerly called Eskimos, living in the far North of the country; and the **First Nations**; and the First Nations, which takes in a wide variety of languages and ethnic backgrounds, and are scattered throughout the country (most prominently in Ontario, BC and the Prairies).

25 Five unique festivals

Festival du Voyageur, Winnipeg (early Feb). Western event honouring the heritage of French fur trappers and traders with traditional cuisine, songs, and events.

Winterlude, Ottawa (Feb). Held over most of the month, a chilly but fun celebration with ice skating, winter rides, quirky events and majestic snow and ice sculptures.

Calgary Stampede (early July). Rollicking Western event with plenty of cowboy attire, downhome eats, and, of course, high-kicking rodeo events.

Celtic Roots Festival, Goderich, ON (early Aug). The culture of Celtic Scotland, Wales and Ireland celebrated in its Canadian form – especially good for folk music.

Canadian National Exhibition, Toronto (late Aug). Huge agricultural fair with rides, clowns, food and music, and sculptures made from rocks, sand, and butter.

Ultimate
experiences
Canada
small print

ROUGH GUIDES – don't just travel

We hope you've been inspired by the experiences in this book. To us, they sum up what makes Canada such an extraordinary and stimulating place to travel. There are 24 other books in the 25 Ultimate Experiences series, each conceived to whet your appetite for travel and for everything the world has to offer. As well as covering the globe, the 25s series also includes books on **Journeys, World Food, Adventure Travel, Places to Stay, Ethical Travel, Wildlife Adventures** and **Wonders of the World**.

When you start planning your trip, Rough Guides' new-look guides, maps and phrasebooks are the ultimate companions. For 25 years we've been refining what makes a good guidebook and we now include more colour photos and more information – on average 50% more pages – than any of our competitors. Just look for the sky-blue spines.

Rough Guides don't just travel – we also believe in getting the most out of life without a passport. Since the publication of the bestselling Rough Guides to **The Internet** and **World Music**, we've brought out a wide range of lively and authoritative guides on everything from **Climate Change** to **Hip-Hop**, from **MySpace** to **Film Noir** and from **The Brain** to **The Rolling Stones**.

Publishing information

Rough Guide 25 Ultimate experiences Canada Published May 2007 by Rough Guides Ltd, 80 Strand, London WC2R 0RL
345 Hudson St, 4th Floor,
New York, NY 10014, USA
14 Local Shopping Centre, Panchsheel Park, New Delhi 110017, India
Distributed by the Penguin Group
Penguin Books Ltd,
80 Strand, London WC2R 0RL
Penguin Group (USA)
375 Hudson Street, NY 10014, USA
Penguin Group (Australia)
250 Camberwell Road, Camberwell, Victoria 3124, Australia
Penguin Books Canada Ltd,
10 Alcorn Avenue, Toronto, Ontario, Canada M4V 1E4
Penguin Group (NZ)
67 Apollo Drive, Mairangi Bay, Auckland 1310, New Zealand

Printed in China
© Rough Guides 2007
No part of this book may be reproduced in any form without permission from the publisher except for the quotation of brief passages in reviews.
80pp
A catalogue record for this book is available from the British Library
ISBN: 978-1-84353-817-2
The publishers and authors have done their best to ensure the accuracy and currency of all the information in **Rough Guide 25 Ultimate experiences Canada**, however, they can accept no responsibility for any loss, injury, or inconvenience sustained by any traveller as a result of information or advice contained in the guide.

1   3   5   7   9   8   6   4   2

Rough Guide credits

Editors: Andrew Rosenberg, Steven Horak, Anna Owens
Design: Henry Iles
Picture research: Jeremy Williams
Cartography: Katie Lloyd-Jones, Maxine Repath

Cover design: Diana Jarvis, Chloë Roberts
Production: Aimee Hampson, Katherine Owers
Proofreader: Steven Horak

The authors

Janine Israel (Experiences 1, 5, 9, 13, 18, 25) has lived in Vancouver and contributes to the Rough Guide to Canada.
Felicity Aston (Experiences 2, 20) leads wintertime adventure expeditions and contributes to the Rough Guide to Canada.
Phil Lee (Experiences 3, 6, 23) is co-author of Rough Guides to Toronto and Canada.
Ross Velton (Experience 4) lives in Montréal and contributes to numerous Rough Guides.
Christian Williams (Experiences 7, 8, 10, 12, 14, 16, 17, 24) is co-author of Rough Guides to Canada and Skiing & Snowboarding in North America.
Megan McIntyre (Experiences 11, 19) spent a year travelling Canada, feeding her passion for maple syrup, ice-hockey and Anne of Green Gables.
Claus Vogel (Experiences 15, 21) teaches in the Great North and has contributed to the Rough Guide to Canada.
Oliver Marshall (Experience 22) has visited every Canadian province except Newfoundland, and means to get there eventually.

Anna Roberts Welles (Experience 23) has travelled extensively in Maritime Canada. **Jeff Dickey** (Miscellany) lives in the Pacific Northwest, authors numerous Rough Guides and makes frequent trips to British Columbia.

Picture credits

Cover Little Doe Lake in Alonquin Provincial Park © Cosmo Condina/Getty Images

2 Hockey game © Andrew Wallace/Reuters/Corbis

6 Indianer Zelte Tipis © Arco Images/Alamy

8–9 Stanley Park and Vancouver skyline © Tim Thompson/Corbis

10–11 Mingan Archipelago © Alain Dumas; Two kayakers © Guy Moberly/Alamy

12–13 Boy running on the beach © L. Rathkelly/MaXx Images Inc

14–15 Montréal © Andre Jenny/Alamy; Star image © Henry Iles

16–17 Lake Louise, Rockies in background © Paul A Souders/Corbis

18–19 Maid of the Mist, Niagara Falls © Kelly-Mooney Photography/Corbis

20–21 Polar bears crossing snowfield © John Conrad/Corbis

22–23 Vieux-Québec at dusk in winter © Richard T Nowitz/Corbis

24–25 Front Street, Dawson City © Museum of History and Industry/Corbis

26–27 Calgary Stampede © Johan Lundberg/Corbis

28–29 Dundas Street, Chinatown © Bill Brooks/Alamy; Chinese restaurant in Toronto © Robert Fried/Alamy

30–31 Heliskiers on mountainside © Karl Weatherly/Corbis

32–33 Tea at Empress Hotel © Carl & Ann Purcell/Corbis

34–35 Aurora borealis © Stock Connection/Alamy

36–37 Canoeing on misty morning © Benjamin Rondel/Corbis

38–39 Hockey game © Andrew Wallace/Reuters/Corbis

40–41 Mountains overlooking Icefields Parkway © Phil Schermeister

42–43 Haida totem pole detail © britishcolumbiaphotos.com

44–45 Train passing grain elevator © Paul A Souders/Corbis

46–47 P'tit Train du Nord bike path © Megapress/Alamy; Leaf images © Henry Iles

48–49 Humphback whale fluke © W Perry Conway/Corbis; Puffin © Bob Krist/Corbis

50–51 Indianer Zelte Tipis © Arco Images/Alamy

52–53 Eroded rocks on Shepody Bay Beach, at head of Bay of Fundy © Paul A Souders/Corbis

54–55 Manitou Lake © Jtb Photo Communications Inc

56–57 Winter surfing © Christopher J Morris/Corbis

58 Polar bears crossing snowfield © John Conrad/Corbis

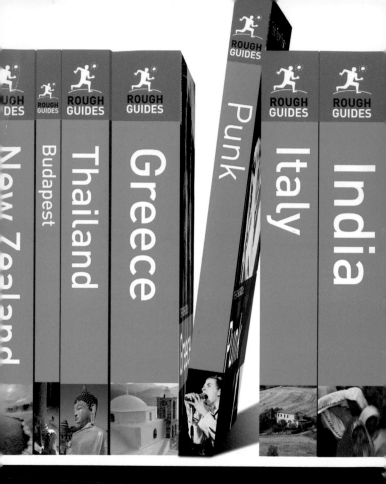

ROUGH GUIDES

New Zealand

Budapest

Thailand

Greece

Punk

ROUGH GUIDES

Italy

India

Over 70 reference books and hundreds of travel
guides, maps & phrasebooks that cover the world.